REAS

PHILOSOPHICAL WORKS

GABRIELLE-ÉMILIE DE BRETEUIL,

MARQUISE DU CHÂTELET

A.K.A.

ÉMILIE DU CHÂTELET

(1706–49)

TRANSLATED BY

KIRK WATSON

2019

Contents

TRANSLATOR'S INTRODUCTION 3

FOUNDATIONS OF PHYSICS: FOREWORD 7

ON THE PRINCIPLES OF OUR KNOWLEDGE ...23

ON THE EXISTENCE OF GOD 42

ON LIBERTY 60

TRANSLATOR'S PREFACE TO MANDEVILLE'S *FABLE OF THE BEES* 81

ON THE RESURRECTION OF THE DEAD 94

ON HAPPINESS 98

TRANSLATOR'S INTRODUCTION

Émilie du Châtelet (1706-49) was a mathematician, an experimental scientist and member of scientific academies, a popular author, a translator of Newton, the popularizer of Leibniz, a philosopher, a socialite, and more. Born into nobility, with parents who encouraged her talents, Émilie was educated by the best minds and raised in the company of the influential figures of the age. She developed close relationships with the central thinkers of the Enlightenment, the most important of which was Voltaire, and she had friendships, romantic attachments, correspondence, influence, or patronage relationships with many others, including La Mettrie, Fontenelle, Maupertuis, Diderot, Saint-Lambert.

From her own day to the present, du Châtelet has been much praised and little read; this small collection offers some of her philosophical works, dealing with human knowledge, ethics, equality of the sexes, free-will, God, and religion.

The first three selections are the early chapters in her book *Foundations of Physics*: the Foreword, which Voltaire called "a masterpiece of reason and eloquence", and two chapters called "On the Principles of our Knowledge" and "On the Existence of God". Her *Foundations of Physics* was an "original synthesis of Cartesian and Leibnizian metaphysics and Newtonian mechanics" and was immediately praised in European scientific journals[1]. It was also furtively used by many articles in Diderot's *Encyclopedia*. In this book, du Châtelet writes as a mother teaching this science to an adolescent.

Next, "On Liberty" was a product of her intense period of collaboration with her longtime companion Voltaire, and, like much of her work from this time, was originally attributed to him. This text is an effort to refute several objections to human free-will. Since "all of morality" is at stake in this

---

[1] Judith P. Zinsser. "Betrayals: An Eighteenth-Century Philosophe and Her Biographers." *French Historical Studies* (2016) 39 (1): p. 4. https://doi-org.ezproxy.lib.utah.edu/10.1215/00161071-3323421

question, the truth is of utmost importance. Human freedom is a "self-moving power" inherent in humans and felt intensely by them.

Her "Translator's Preface to Mandeville's Fable of the Bees" opens with autobiographical musings and discusses institutional limitations she faced as a woman. She also shares her ideas on the craft and the usefulness of translation, suggesting it as a valid intellectual vocation. She concludes with a few words on her text ("the best book of morality that has ever been written") and her author (the "English Montaigne", only better).

Next, the brief "On the Resurrection of the Dead", is a skeptical rewriting of a text from Abbot Calmet's contemporary Biblical commentary. This text represents a tiny but interesting excerpt from du Châtelet's own commentary, *Examens de la Bible*. She begins by calling the resurrection of the dead "one of the most absurd things that men have ever imagined".

The final selection, "On Happiness", might be thought of as du Châtelet's testament, a somewhat melancholy report of her own mixed results in attaining love and happiness.

As her contribution to ethics, it presents a kind of hedonism: all happiness comes from sensations, maximizing pleasure is the highest good: "We are only happy as a result of strong and pleasant sensations"; "Happiness comes only through the satisfaction of our tastes and passions". In what seems an unlikely statement from such a rational thinker, du Châtelet also claims that "illusions" are necessary for happiness: they do for the soul what the brain does with the sight, adapting outside objects to our nature for our purposes. Without illusions providing this gloss on our relationships with others, unvarnished realities would leave us too cold and alone in the universe.

FOUNDATIONS OF PHYSICS: FOREWORD

From *Foundations of Physics*

I.

I have always thought that the most sacred duty of men was to give their children an education that would prevent them, when they were older, from regretting their youth, which is the only time when one can truly get an education; you, my dear son, have now arrived at this happy age when the mind begins to think, and when the heart isn't yet subject to those intense emotions that will later come to disturb it.

The present moment may be the only time in your life when you can devote yourself to the study of nature, soon the emotions and the distractions of your age will consume all of your time; and when this flight of youth has passed, and you have paid to the world's intoxication the tribute of your age and state, ambition will take hold of your soul; even in this more advanced age, which is often no more mature, you may wish to apply yourself to the Study of the true Sciences, your mind then having lost this suppleness of youth, you will then have to strive, with toilsome Studies, for what you might learn today with great ease. Therefore, I would have you put to good use the dawn of your reason, and try to secure yourself from the ignorance which is still only too common among those of your station, and which is always one failing the more, and one advantage the less.

You must habituate your mind to thinking while you're still young, and to autonomy; you will always sense what help and consolation comes from Studying, and you will see that it may even bring you amusement and pleasure.

II.

The study of physics seems to be made for man, based as it is on things that are constantly around us, on which our pleasures and needs depend: I will strive, in this Work, to bring this Science within your reach, and separate it from this admirable art called Algebra, which, by separating things from images, hides away from the senses, and only addresses itself to the understanding: you are not yet ready to understand this Language, which seems more like that of the Intelligences than of Men, it is reserved for study in later years than now; but truth can take different forms, and here I will try to give it one suitable to your age, and to tell you only about things that can be understood with the help of the common Geometry that you have studied.

Never cease, my son, to cultivate this Science which you have learned from your earliest youth; without its help it would be vain to think we could make much progress in the study of Nature, it is the key to all discovery; and if many things remain unexplained in Physics, this is only because we have not applied ourselves to delve into them with Geometry, and because nobody has yet taken this Science far enough.

III.

I am often amazed that as many capable people as France possesses have not beat me to the task that I am undertaking today for you, for I must admit that, although we have many excellent books on Physics in French, yet we have no complete course in Physics, aside from the small *Treatise* by Rohaut, which is eighty years old; but this *Treatise*, while quite good for the time in which it was composed, has become quite inadequate in light of how many discoveries have been made since then: and a man who has only studied Physics in that one Book would still have much to learn.

As for me, while deploring this state of indigence, I am far from thinking myself capable of making up the difference, in this Work I intend to do nothing but gather before your eyes the discoveries that are found scattered in so many Latin, Italian, and English books; most of the truths they contain are known by few French Readers, and I would save you the trouble of searching them out in these sources, whose profundity might intimidate and discourage you.

IV.

Although the work I am undertaking requires much time and effort, I will regret none of the troubles it costs me, and I will think it well used if it can inspire you with a love of the

Sciences, and the desire to cultivate your reason. What trouble and effort people expend every day in the uncertain hope of winning honors and increasing the wealth of their children! Is the knowledge of the truth and the habit of searching it out and following it, any less worthy of my attention? Especially in an age where a taste for Physics is found in all parts of society, and has begun to be united with the other sciences of the world?

V.

I won't relate the history of the various revolutions in Physics; the whole story of these would fill a large Volume; I intend to share with you, *less what has been thought than what must be known.*

Until the last century, the Sciences were an impenetrable secret, in which only the so-called Savants were initiated, it was a kind of Cabal, whose password consisted in various barbaric words apparently devised to confuse and repel the mind.

Descartes appeared in this dark night like a Star giving light to the universe, the revolution that this great man brought to the Sciences is surely more useful, and is perhaps even more noteworthy than that of the greatest Empires, and it might be said that human reason is more indebted to Descartes than to anyone else; for, it is far easier to find the truth when you're on its tracks than to depart those of error. This great man's *Geometry*, his *Dioptrics*, his *Method*, are masterpieces of sagacity which will immortalize his name, and if he is mistaken on some points in Physics, this is because he was a man, and no single man, nor any one century can know everything.

We raise ourselves to the knowledge of the truth like those Giants who scaled the Heavens by standing on each other's backs. Descartes and Galileo produced Huygens and Leibniz, these great men whose names you don't yet know, and whose works I will soon teach you, and it was by taking advantage of Kepler's labors, and by using Huygens' Theorems, that Newton was able to discover this universal force spread through all of Nature, which makes the Planets circle around the Sun, and which makes things heavy on earth.

VI.

The systems of Descartes and Newton presently divide the world of thinkers, and so it is necessary for you to understand both of them; but, so many learned men have taught and rectified the system of Descartes that it will be easy for you to become acquainted with it in their books: one of my aims in the first part of this one is to set before your eyes the other party in this great trial, and acquaint you with the system of Mr. Newton, to show you how far he takes his connections and probabilities, and how Phenomena can be explained with the hypothesis of attraction.

You may find much information on this subject in *Elements of Newton's Philosophy*, published last year; and I would omit my own thoughts on this subject, if its illustrious Author had covered more ground; but he restricts himself so narrowly that I can't avoid discussing it.

VII.

My son, whatever side you take in this Philosophers' debate, you must avoid the stubbornness that inevitably comes with party loyalty: this is dangerous in all parts of life, but in Physics it is simply ridiculous; the search for truth is the only place where patriotism should never prevail; and it's surely quite inappropriate for some sort of national affair to be made of Newton's and Descartes's views: when presented with a book on Physics, we should ask whether it is good, not whether its author is English, German, or French.

Moreover, it seems that it would be no less unjust for the Cartesians to disallow attraction as a hypothesis, than for some Newtonians to make it an original property of matter; we must admit that some of them have gone too far on this point, and that there is some justice the criticism that they're like a man with bad eyes who can't see the ropes holding the actors at the Opera, and who, when he sees Bellerophon hanging in mid-air, says: *Bellerophon is hanging in mid-air because he is equally attracted on all sides by the four parts of the stage*, since, to say that the effects attributed by the Newtonians to attraction don't come from momentum, one would have to know every way in which momentum can be employed, but we are still far from this knowledge.

In Physics we are still like the man born blind, whose sight was restored by Dr. Cheselden; at first, this man only saw chaos: he could only grope his way, and after a considerable length of time he finally began to see clearly; this time has not yet entirely come for us, and it may never do so entirely; some truths, it seems, are not meant to be perceived by the eyes of our mind, just as our bodies will never see some objects; but, anyone who refuses to learn from this realization is like a cripple with a fever who refused all medicine only because it wouldn't fix his limp.

VIII.

One of the offenses of some Philosophers of our times is seeking to banish Hypotheses from Physics; these are as necessary for it as Scaffolding is for the construction of a house; yes, when this Building is complete the Scaffolding becomes useless, but it could never have been built without its help. All of Astronomy, for Example, is only based on Hypotheses, and if they had always been avoided in Physics, far fewer discoveries would have been made; nothing, then, could slow the progress of the Sciences more than banishing these, and thinking that we have discovered the grand spring that drives all of nature forward, for we will never look for a cause that we think we already know, and this causes the application of the geometrical principles of Mechanics to Physical effects, which is very difficult and very necessary, to remain imperfect, and we would find ourselves deprived of the labors and research of many great geniuses who might have been capable of discovering the true cause of Phenomena.

It is true that Hypotheses become the poison of Philosophy when they are taken as truths, and they may then become even more dangerous than the unintelligible Scholastic jargon; for, since this jargon was absolutely meaningless, all it took was a little attention for a sound mind to see through its absurdity, and look for the truth elsewhere; but, an ingenious and bold Hypothesis, which has some plausibility at first glance, attracts our human pride to believe it, and the mind applauds itself for having discovered these subtle principles, and then employs all of its sagacity in defending them. Most of the great men who have constructed Systems provide us with Examples of this, which are great Ships pulled by the currents: they make amazing maneuvers, but the current is what really moves them.

IX.

Remember, my son, in all your Studies, that Experience is the baton which was given to us, the blind, to guide us in our quest; with its help we cover much ground, but we will certainly fall if we neglect it; Experience will teach us about the Physical qualities, while our reason will use it, and gain new knowledge and intelligence from it.

X.

If I have found it necessary to warn you about the party loyalty, I must also recommend that you should never bring your respect for the greatest of men to the point of Idolatry, as many of their disciples do; each Philosopher has seen something, and none has seen the whole; and no book is so bad that it has nothing to teach us, and none are so good that there is nothing to criticize in them. When I read Aristotle, this Philosopher who has endured such a diverse and unjust fate, I am shocked to sometimes find ideas that are so sound on so many points of general Physics, alongside utter nonsense, and when I read some of the questions that Newtown placed at the end of his Optics, I am struck by a rather different sort of astonishment: this Example of the two greatest men of their respective eras must show you that when we have the use of our reason, we should not take anyone at their word, but always examine for ourselves, brushing aside all esteem for famous names.

XI.

This is one of the reasons why I have not filled this book with citations, I have not wished to win you over with authorities; and besides, there are already too many of these; I am far from believing myself capable of writing a book of Physics without consulting any books at all, and I doubt that anyone could write a good one without some outside help. The greatest Philosopher can add new discoveries to those of others, but once a truth is discovered, he must adhere to it, and Newton, for Example, found it necessary to begin by establishing Kepler's two Analogies when he set out to explain the paths of the Planets, without which he would never have made the discovery of stellar gravitation.

Physics is an immense Building, beyond the power of a single man; some only manage to set a single stone, while others build entire wings, but all must work on the solid foundations which have been laid for this Building in the last century, with Geometry and Observation; there are others who hold up the Building's Plan, and which is precisely what I do.

In this Book I have not focused on being witty, but being right; and I have enough regard for your own wit to expect you will be capable of seeking the truth independently of all the foreign ornamentation that has been lavished on it in our time. I have been content to remove the thorns which might hurt your delicate hands, but I have made no efforts to replace them with exotic flowers, and I am sure that a good mind, as feeble as it may still be, will find greater pleasure, and a more satisfying one, in clear and precise reasoning which it can easily grasp, than in misplaced banter.

XII.

I teach you, in the first Chapters of this book, the main ideas of Mr. Leibniz on Metaphysics; I have taken these from the Works of the famous Wolff[2], with one of whose Disciples you have so often heard me in conversation, who has spent time in my home, and who sometimes provided me with extracts from his master.

Leibniz's metaphysical ideas are, as yet, little known in France, but they surely deserve to be known: despite this great man's discoveries, much of Metaphysics remains obscure; but it seems that he has furnished us, in his principle of sufficient reason, with a compass to guide us along the shifting sands of this science.

That thick fogs still cover some parts of Metaphysics has served as a pretext for the laziness of most men to avoid studying it, who tell themselves that, since not everything is known, nothing can be known; but there are

---

[2] See Wolf's *Ontology*, especially the following Chapters: *De Principia Contradictionis, de Principia Rationis Sufficientis, de Possibili, & Impossibili, de Necessaria & Contingente, de Extensione, Continuitate, Spatio, Tempore,* etc.

certainly some parts of Metaphysics that can be demonstrated, less rigorously than geometrical demonstrations, although they're of a different kind: we lack a calculus for Metaphysics to match what has been discovered for Geometry, by means of which, with the help of some *data*, we are able to know *unknowns*; perhaps some genius will discover this calculus someday. Mr. Leibniz has expended considerable thought on this point, and he harbored certain ideas about it, but unfortunately he never shared them with anyone. Even when this is discovered, it seems that certain unknowns will still remain, the *equations* of will never be discovered. Metaphysics contains two kinds of things; first, that which all people who make good use of their minds can know, and secondly and more extensively, that which they will never know.

Many of the truths of Physics, Metaphysics, and Geometry are evidently intertwined. Metaphysics is the pinnacle of the building; but this pinnacle is so high in the air that it can be hard to make out. I have, therefore, thought it necessary to start by bringing it into your field of vision, so that no cloud will be in your way, and you can see, clearly and securely, the truths I would like to introduce to you.

ON THE PRINCIPLES OF OUR KNOWLEDGE

From *Foundations of Physics*

I.

All of our Knowledge comes from other Knowledge, and is based on certain Principles, the truth of which is known without reflection, being self-evident.

There are truths that relate immediately to these first Principles, and which only follow from them through a small number of deductions; then the mind can easily see the links connecting them; but it is easy to lose sight of these in the search for truths to which can only be found across a great number of deductions derived from each other. We find countless examples of this in Geometry; it is quite easy, for example, to see that the Diameter of a Circle divides it into two equal parts, since it only takes a single deduction to come from the nature of a Circle to this property; but it is not so easy to see that the square of the ordinate BM is equal to the rectangle of Line AB via Line BC, even though this property follows from the nature of a Circle just like the first one, since many intermediate deductions must be drawn before we can arrive at this last property. Therefore, it is very important to pay attention to these Principles, and to the way truths follow from them, if we want to stay right.

II.

This word Principle has suffered much abuse; the Scholastics, who never demonstrated anything, took unintelligible words as their principles. Descartes, who realized how greatly this way of reasoning separated men from truth, began by establishing that we should only reason on the basis of clear ideas; but he took this principle too far, since he accepts the possibility of appealing to a certain intense feeling of clarity and evidence to ground our reasoning.

When following this principle, this Philosopher went awry on the essence of Body, which he said consisted in extension alone, since he thought extension offered a clear and distinct idea of Body, without bothering to prove the possibility of this idea that we'll soon see is very incomplete, since we must add to it the force of inertia and the active force. This method, moreover, would only render the disputes eternal, since, every party with a distinct opinion has their own intense and internal sense of what they advance; and therefore none would have to submit, having equal evidence on their side; therefore, we must replace the illusions of our imaginations with demonstrations, and nothing should be considered true but what follows incontestably from the first principles which nobody can question, and reject as false all that is contrary to these principles, or against the truths that have been established by their means, no matter what may be imagined about them.

III.

Even slight attention to procedure in Science, where uncertainty rises to its apex, will be enough to show the utility of this method. There is no clearer idea, for example, than the idea of the possibility of an equilateral triangle, and that if you add the two sides of a triangle they will be longer than the third one:

however, Euclid, this strict thinker, was not content to rely on some intense and internal opinion that we have of these truths, but he demonstrated them rigorously, showing how one must proceed to construct an equilateral triangle, and that it would be a contradiction if the two sides of a triangle put together weren't larger than the third.

IV.

We call anything that affirms and denies the same thing at the same time a *contradiction*; this principle is the first Axiom on which all truths are based. Everyone readily grants this, and it would even be impossible to deny it without lying to one's own conscience; since we know that we cannot force our mind to believe that something is and is not at the same time, and that we can't not have an idea while we do have it, or see a white Body as black, when we see it as white. Even the Pyrrhonians, who professed to doubt everything, never denied this principle; yes, they denied that there was any reality in things, but they didn't doubt that they had an idea when they did have one.

This Axiom is the foundation of all certainty in human knowledge; for, if we agreed that something can both exist and not exist at the same time, there would be no room for any truth, even in numbers, and everything could be, or not be, as each fancied, and thus, 2 x 2 could equal either 4 or 6, or both at the same time.

V.

From what has just been said, it follows that the impossible is that which involves a contradiction, and the possible is that which does not. Many Philosophers define the possible and the impossible differently, and consider impossible that which gives no clear and distinct idea, and possible that which can be conceived, and which is attached to a corresponding clear idea. This definition, if properly explained, could be accepted; but we must be careful lest it lead us to take mistaken and deceptive notions for clear notions: for we often form mistaken ideas which only seem obvious because we're not paying attention...

Therefore, to avoid error we must verify our ideas, demonstrate their reality, and only consider them as beyond doubt when we are assured by experience or by demonstration that they contain nothing false or illusory.

VI.

The above definition of the impossible entails a very important rule, namely, that when we make the claim that something is impossible, we must show that someone is both denying and affirming the same thing at the same time, or that it is contrary to a truth that has already been demonstrated. This rule would prevent many disputes if followed; for it would immediately remove all doubt from all propositions, and show the inadequacy of the proofs of those who call whatever doesn't fit with their opinions, impossible.

We must take the same precautions to ensure that something is possible; for, we must be in a position to demonstrate that it involves no contradiction: without this condition, our ideas are only opinions with degrees of probability, which offer no certainty.

VII.

The principle of contradiction has always been used in Philosophy. Aristotle, and all Philosophers after him have used it, and Descartes used it in his Philosophy to prove that we exist: for, if anyone doubts their own existence, this in itself would certainly be a proof of their existence, since it would be a contradiction if they had any idea at all, including a doubt, while not existing.

This principle is sufficient for all necessary truths, that is, for the truths that can only be determined in one way, for this is what the term *necessary* means; but in the case of contingent truths, that is, when something can exist in different ways, and none of its determinations are more necessary than others, the need for another principle arises, since that of contradiction vanishes. Thus, the Ancients, who were unaware of this fertile principle of our knowledge, were mistaken about the most important points of Philosophy.

VIII.

This principle, on which all contingent truths depend, and which is no less primitive or universal than that of contradiction, is the *principle of sufficient reason:* all men follow this naturally; since nobody chooses to do one thing and not another without a sufficient reason why it is preferable to its alternative.

When we ask someone to account for their actions, we interrogate them until we find a satisfactory reason, and in all matters we feel unable to force our mind to affirm something without a sufficient reason, that is, without a reason that makes us understand why this thing is so rather than otherwise.

If anyone were to deny this great principle, they would fall into strange contradictions: for, if we allow that something can happen without a sufficient reason, we cannot be sure of anything, that anything is the same from one moment to the next, since anything could change, at any moment, into something else entirely; then, there would be no truths for us outside of the present moment.

I might claim, for example, that everything is still in my room just as I left it, because I am sure that nobody has been there since I went away; but if the principle of sufficient reason did not apply, all my certainty becomes an illusion, since there might well be a mess in my room without anyone having gone in and moved anything around.

Without this principle there would be no identical things; for, two things are identical when they can take each other's place without any change to the property in question. This definition is universally accepted; so, for example, if I have a ball of stone and a ball of lead, and I can replace one with the other in the trays of a scale, without the scales going up or down, then I say that the weights of these balls is identical, that it is the same, and that they are identical in their weight: but, if something could happen without a sufficient reason, then I couldn't pronounce the weight of these balls as identical at the same moment as I affirm it to be identical; since a change might happen without any reason in one with no corresponding change in the other; and consequently, their weight would no longer be identical, which is contrary to the definition.

Without the principle of sufficient reason, we could not say that this Universe, all of whose parts are so closely interconnected, could only have been produced by a supreme wisdom; for, if effects could occur without sufficient reason, then everything could have been produced by chance, that is, by nothing.

What often occurs in dreams gives us an idea of a fabulous world where everything happens without sufficient reason.

I dream that I am busy writing in my room; suddenly my chair changes into a winged horse, and I find myself a hundred leagues away, and mingling with people who are long dead, etc. None of this can happen in our world, since there is no sufficient reason for all these effects; since, when I leave my room, I can say how and why I leave, and I don't go from one place to another without passing through the space in between: but, all these illusions would equally be possible if effects could exist without sufficient reason: this principle is what distinguishes dreams from waking life and the real world from the fabulous one of fairy tales. Thus, those who deny the principle of sufficient reason are living in a fabulous world that does not exist; but in this one, everything must happen according to this principle.

In Geometry, where all truths are necessary ones, only the principle of contradiction is used: since, for example, the sum of a triangle's angles can only be determined in one way, and they must absolutely be equal to two right angles; but, if it is possible for something to be in different states, I cannot claim that it is in one state rather than another, at least as long as I provide no reason to back up my claims: thus, for example, I can be seated, lying, or standing: all these positions are equally possible, but when I am standing, there must be a sufficient reason why I am standing, and not sitting or lying down.

Archimedes, while transitioning from Geometry to Mechanics, recognized the need for sufficient reason; since, when he tried to demonstrate that a scales with arms in equal balance will remain balanced, he showed that in this equality of its arms and weights, the scales must remain at rest, because there would be no sufficient reason for one of its arms to descend and not the other one.

Mr. Leibniz, who was quite attentive to the sources of our reasoning, grasped this principle, developed it, and was the first to distinctly pronounce it, and he introduced it into Science.

We must allow that no greater service could be hoped for, since most false reasoning has no other source than neglect of sufficient reason; and you will soon see that this principle is the only thread that can guide us in these labyrinths of error which the human mind has built for the pleasure of wandering there.

Therefore, we should accept nothing that violates this fundamental axiom, this bridle for the imagination, which makes countless deviations when we don't subject it to the rules of severe reasoning.

IX.

We must distinguish clearly between the possible and the actual. You have already seen that anything that would not involve a contradiction is possible; but it is not actual. It is possible, for example, for this square table to become round; but it may also never happen; therefore, since all that exists is necessarily possible, we may draw a deduction from existence to possibility, but not from possibility to existence.

For something to be, it is not enough for it to be possible, this possibility must also have its accomplishment, which we call *Existence*: and, nothing may come into existence without a sufficient reason, by which an Intelligent Being could understand why this thing becomes actual instead of only possible. Therefore, a cause must contain, not only the principle of actuality of the thing whose cause it is, but also the sufficient reason for this thing, that is, that whereby an intelligent Being can comprehend why it exists: for, nobody with the use of reason should be content to simply know that such a thing is possible, and that it exists, but they should also know the reason why it exists; and if they don't see this reason, as is common enough in complicated matters, they must at least be assured that nobody can demonstrate that the thing in question cannot have a sufficient reason for its existence; and so, there must be, in all that exists, something whereby one can comprehend why that which is was able to exist, and this is called the *sufficient reason*.

X.

This principle banishes from Philosophy all the reasoning of the Scholastics; for, while the Scholastics allowed that nothing happens without a cause, they point to plastic natures, vegetative souls, and other words devoid of meaning as causes; but when it is established that a cause only suffices to the extent that it satisfies the principle of sufficient reason, that is, to the extent that it contains something by which one can show how and why an effect can happen, then one can no longer employ these big words that have been used instead of Ideas.

When someone sets out, for example, to explain why Plants are born, grow, and survive, and they attribute these effects to a vegetative soul found in all Plants, they are making an unacceptable claim, which offers nothing that will help me understand how this growth occurs; for, even if we posit this vegetative soul, it doesn't help us understand why any given Plant has one structure and not another, or how this soul can form a Machine like that of this Plant.

XI.

The principle of sufficient reason is also the basis for the rules and customs which are only grounded on what is called *decorum*, for the same men could follow different customs, they could decide to act in many ways; and when one chooses, in preference to others, those based on better reasons, these actions become good and cannot be criticized; but they are called unreasonable when there are sufficient reasons to avoid doing so, and on the basis of the same principles, we can pronounce one custom better than another, that is, when they have more reason on their side.

XII.

From this great Axiom of sufficient reason there follows another which Leibniz calls *the principle of Indiscernibles*: this principle banishes from the universe all similar matter, for if two parts of matter were absolutely similar and alike, and one bit could be replaced by another without the least alteration (for this is what "entirely similar" means), there would be no sufficient reason why one of these particles would be located in the Moon, for example, and the other on Earth, since, by trading their places and locating what is on the Moon on Earth, and what is on the Earth on the Moon, everything would remain the same. We are, therefore, obliged to recognize that even the slightest parts of matter are discernable, or that each of them is infinitely different from all the rest, and that each could not be used anywhere else without deranging the order of the whole universe. Thus, each particle of matter is destined to have the effect that it produces, and this is the source of diversity, which is no less present between two grains of sand than between our Globe and that of Saturn, which shows that the wisdom of the Creator is no less astounding in the tiniest Being than in the largest one.

This infinite diversity, which is so prevalent in nature, presents itself to us everywhere our senses can reach. Mr. Leibniz, who was the first to teach this truth, had the pleasure of seeing it confirmed by those who denied it, during a stroll with the Electress of Hanover, in the Gardens of Herrenhausen: this Philosopher claimed that nobody would ever find two leaves that are completely alike in their almost infinite quantity, and many of the courtiers then present wasted much of the day trying to disprove his theory, but they were unable to find two leaves without clear and visible differences.

There are other objects which look similar to us only because they're small, since we don't see them distinctly, but microscopes show us how variegated they really are: in addition, experiments, which aren't necessary in this case, also confirm this principle.

XIII.

From this Axiom of sufficient reason follows yet another principle which has been called *the Law of continuity*, and again it is to Leibniz that we owe this principle, which is of so fecund in Physics; it teaches us that nothing happens by leaps in nature, and that no Being can pass from one state to another without passing through all the different states that might be conceived as lying between them.

The principle of sufficient reason easily proves this truth, for every state in which a Being finds itself must have its sufficient reason why said Being is in this state rather than another one, and this reason can only be found in its prior state. This prior state therefore contained something which brought about the subsequent, present state, and the two states are so closely connected that it is impossible to place another state between them: for, if another state were possible between the current state and the one immediately prior, then nature would have left the first state without being yet driven by the second one to abandon the first; there would, therefore, be no sufficient reason why it should pass to this state instead of any other possible state; thus, no Being passes from one state to another without passing through the intermediary states, just as nobody goes from one City to another without traveling along the road in between...

It's the same in nature as in Geometry, and it was not without good cause that Plato called the Creator *the Eternal Geometer.* Thus, in nature there are no angles, strictly speaking, no sudden inflections or rebounding; but there is gradation in all things, and everything is prepared long before for the changes that it will undergo, and everything goes gradually to the state that it must assume...

XIV.

It is by this law of continuity that the true laws of motion can be discovered and demonstrated, since a body that moves in any direction cannot move in the opposite direction without first going from its original state of motion to rest via all the intermediate degrees of deceleration to rest, and then going back, by imperceptible degrees of acceleration, from rest to this new motion...

ON THE EXISTENCE OF GOD

From *Foundations of Physics*

The study of nature elevates us to the knowledge of a Supreme Being. This great truth is even more necessary, if possible, for good physics than morality, and it must be the foundation and the conclusion of all our efforts in this science.

Therefore, I find it indispensable to begin by placing before your eyes a summary of the proofs of this important truth, by which you can make your own ruling with the evidence before you.

Something exists, since I exist.

Since something exists, something must have existed from all eternity; otherwise nothingness, which is only a negation, would have produced all that exists; which is a contradiction in terms, since this would mean that something has been produced, without recognizing any cause for its existence.

The being which has existed from all eternity must have a necessary existence, without any cause for its existence; for, if it had received its existence from another being, this other being must have existed by itself; and then this would be the one I'm talking about, and this is God; or it would have its existence from still another. It's easy to see that, by an infinite regression like this, we must come to a necessary being which exists by itself, or else admit an infinite chain of beings, which, taken together, would have no external cause for their existence (since all beings are part of this infinite chain), and which, each in particular, have no internal cause, since none of them exist by themselves, and they all have their existence as part of an infinite gradation. To assume a chain of beings like this which, separately, were produced by a cause, and which, all together, were produced by nothing, is a contradiction in terms. Therefore, there is a being which exists necessarily, since it would be a contradiction for such a being not to exist.

Everything that surrounds us is born and perishes in turn, nothing enjoys a necessary state; everything happens successively, and we ourselves come in succession to each other.

Therefore, there is nothing but contingence in all the beings around us, that is, that the contrary is equally possible, and involves no contradiction (for this is what distinguishes a contingent being from a necessary being).

Everything that exists has a sufficient reason for its existence; thus, the sufficient reason for the existence of a being must lie either within or without itself; and the reason for the existence of a contingent being cannot lie within itself; for, had it contained the sufficient reason for its existence within itself, it would be impossible for it not to exist; which is contrary to the definition of a contingent being. The sufficient reason for the existence of a contingent being must, therefore, necessarily be without itself, since it cannot be within itself.

This sufficient reason cannot be in another contingent being, or in a series of these beings, since the same question would always return at the end of this chain, no matter how extensive it is. Therefore, we must arrive at a necessary being containing the sufficient reason for the existence of all contingent beings and of its own, and this Being is God.

The attributes of this supreme being result from the necessity of its existence.

Thus, it is eternal; i.e., it had no beginning and will never have an end; for, if the necessary being had a beginning, it must either have acted before it existed to produce itself, which is absurd; or else something else must have produced it, which is against the definition of a necessary being.

It can have no end, since, given that the sufficient reason of its existence lies in itself, it can ever abandon it; in addition, that which is contrary to a necessary thing involves a contradiction, and is consequently impossible: it is, therefore, impossible for the necessary being to cease to exist, just as it is impossible for three times three to be equal to eight.

It is immutable: for, if it changed, it would no longer be what it was, and consequently it could not have existed necessarily; in addition, each successive state would require its own sufficient reason in a preceding state, the next in another one, and so on. And, since in the necessary being we will never arrive at the final state, since the being never had a beginning, some successive state would be without a sufficient reason, if it were susceptible to succession; thus, there could be no change or succession in the necessary being.

It clearly follows from what has just been said that the necessary being cannot be a composite being which only exists to the extent that its parts are joined together, and which could be destroyed by the dissociation of these same parts; and consequently, the self-existent being is a simple being.

The world we see cannot be the necessary being, for it is composed of parts, and there is a continual succession within it; which is in absolute contradistinction to the attributes I have just shown as belonging to the necessary being.

For the same reason, neither matter nor the elements of matter can by any means be the necessary being.

Nor can our soul be this necessary being; for its perceptions are continually changing, and it exists in a state of perpetual variation; but the necessary being cannot vary: our soul is, therefore, not the necessary being.

The self-existent being is, therefore, a being different from the world we see, from the matter of which this world is made, from the elements of which matter is made, and from our soul; and it contains in itself the sufficient reason for its existence and that of all beings that exist.

It's easy to see, from all that has been said, that there can only be one necessary being; if there had been two beings existing necessarily and independently of each other, it would be possible for each of them to exist alone, and consequently neither of them would exist necessarily.

It is evident that everything that possible doesn't exist, and that an infinity of things which might happen do not occur. For example, instead of destroying the Persian empire, Alexander might have turned his arms against the Western nations, or even dwelt peaceably in his own kingdom; ultimately, he might have chosen to do an infinite number of different things, all of which would have brought into existence an infinity of combinations which were then possible, and which would have produced entirely different events from those which happened in fact. The events that contained in novels are no different; they could have happened, if another series of events had occurred; these are stories of a possible world, the actuality of which is lacking; for, each series of things constitutes a world that would be different from all the rest, by reason of its own particular events. Thus, we can conceive of the series of causes that conspired to produce the events in the *Zaïde*, or those of the Queen of Navarre, since these events are possible; all they lack is actuality: just as we can conceive of possible universes with other stars and other planets; and since the different relations of this universe can be combined in infinitely different ways, there is an infinity of possible worlds, of which only a single one exists in actuality.

Back when nothing had yet been produced, and none of these possible worlds existed, they were all equally empowered to come into existence; and they awaited, so to speak, for an external power to call upon them and actualize them; for that which does not exist can only contribute to its existence ideally, that is, as far as it contains certain determinations which the rest do not, and which can lead an intelligent being to select it and confer existence on it.

There must be a sufficient reason for the actuality of the visible world, since infinite other worlds were also possible. And this reason can be found nowhere but in the differences that distinguish this world from all other worlds. Therefore, the necessary being must have represented all possible worlds to himself, must have considered their diverse arrangements and differences, in order to decide to give actuality to the one it found most pleasing.

The distinct representation of things is the substance of the understanding: and the necessary being who must have represented to itself all possible worlds before creating this one, is therefore an intelligent being whose understanding is infinite; for, all possible worlds contain all possible arrangements of all possible things. Thus, this being we call God is an intelligent being who sees, not only everything that happens in actuality, but also everything that would happen in every possible combination of things; for, all that is possible is within the worlds that it contemplates without cease, and which play themselves out, so to speak, before its eyes.

Since succession is an imperfection attached to what is finite, there is no succession in the perceptions of God, who sees at once all possible worlds with all possible modifications; and since our ideas contain an infinity of confused things, which we can't disentangle due to their multiplicity, since God's ideas of things are infinitely distinct, they are infinitely different from ours, which is somewhat like our idea of the moon and those of a man who is a longtime resident of it. The way God sees and represents all possible things for himself is, therefore, incomprehensible to us; thus, we can form no distinct idea of the divine understanding; it is, like the creation itself, one of the things that are impossible for us to comprehend and to deny. Let us always remember, when we want to comprehend the understanding of God, that child seen by St. Augustine on the seaside, who was trying to fit the whole sea inside a hazelnut shell; this will give us a pale idea of the presumption of a being whose understanding is finite, but wishes to have a clear idea of the understanding of the Creator.

God's choice, among all possible worlds, of the world we see, is a proof of his liberty; for, having given actuality to a series of things that contribute nothing by their own power to their existence, there is no reason why he cannot give existence to the other possible series; all of which were equal with respect to their possibility. He has, therefore, opted for the series of things which comprise this universe, to actualize it, because it pleases him the most; he was the absolute master of his choice. The necessary being is, therefore, a free being; for, to act by the choice of one's own will is to be free.

But the choice he made of this world was made for some reason; the supreme intelligence does not conduct itself without intelligence. And, since we earthlings expect that a being is more or less intelligent as it is moved by reasons that are more or less sufficient, since God is the most perfect of all beings, none of his actions can be without their sufficient reason. Therefore, he had a reason to decide to create a world, and this reason is the satisfaction he found in communicating a part of his perfections, and the reason which led him to give actuality to this world rather than another was the greater perfection he found in this one. But, this reason is not outside of God or prior to him; he finds it in himself, it is a part of his intelligence; for, since all possible worlds are series of things which are coexistent and successive, these series possess different degrees of perfection as they are more or less connected, and as they tend more or less harmoniously to a general end. And the contemplation of perfection is the source of pleasure for intelligent beings; since that which has the greatest perfection is the most pleasant of things, and a rational being only desires things as it sees them to possess perfections: but, since our understanding is limited, and since we are liable to err in our judgments, we often mistake an apparent perfection for a real perfection; whereas, since God sees things with an infinite understanding, he cannot be deceived by appearances, or choose what is bad, for lack of knowing what is good. He perceived, therefore, among all possible worlds, the best and most perfect one, and this greater perfection is the sufficient reason for the preference he gave to this world above all other possible worlds. The necessary being is, therefore, infinitely wise; for, only a being whose wisdom was infinite could choose the most perfect of things.

The final causes, this fruitful principle in physics, and which some philosophers have tried to banish for very bad reasons, originate in this infinite wisdom of the creator; everything points to a design, and only blindness or a desire not to see, can make us overlook the fact that the creator proposed, in even the least of his works, purposes which he always obtains, which nature ceaselessly strives to execute. Thus, this universe is no chaos, no disordered mass without harmony or interconnections, as some declaimers would have us believe; but all of its parts are arranged with infinite wisdom, and none could be transplanted or moved from their place without harming the perfection of the whole.

While studying nature, we discover a portion of the aims and the artistry of the creator in the construction of this universe. Thus, Virgil was right when he said: *Felix qui potuit rerum cognoscere causas*, since the knowledge of causes raises us up to the creator, and initiates us into the mysteries of his design, showing us the astounding order that predominates throughout the universe, and the relations of these different parts, which are not only necessary relations of positioning like above and below, but are relations of a design, of which the whole carries the imprint; and the older the world gets, the more discoveries men make, and the more signs of design are found in the fabrication of the world and of the smallest of its parts.

This world is, therefore, the best of all possible worlds, where the greatest variety coexists with the greatest order, and where the greatest effects are produced by the simplest laws: this is the universe which occupies the point of the pyramid[3], above which there is nothing, but only an infinity below it, of ever-diminishing perfection, and which were, consequently, unworthy of being selected by an infinitely wise being.

This principle does away with all the objections drawn from the evils seen to predominate in this world; God allows them in the universe since they participate in the best series of possible things, from which they

---

[3] Leibniz, continuing in his *Theodicy* the dialogue between Boetie and Valla, introduces the priest of Apollo, who wants to know the source of Sextus Tarquinius, and who seeks this source in the palace of the Fates, which was a pyramid composed of all possible worlds, in which the best one, the one we're in, where Tarquinius committed the crimes which were the cause of Roman liberty, occupied the point thereof.

could not be taken without removing some perfection from the whole; since the whole universe is interconnected; the least event is related to others which preceded it and to an infinity which depend on it and will emerge from it. Therefore, to judge an event, we must not judge it in isolation and outside of its liaisons and the larger sequence, but we must judge it relative to the whole universe, and from the effects it produces in all places and at all times; for, to judge the perfection of the universe from an apparent evil is to judge a whole painting from a single brush-stroke, and it is an illusion to imagine that all imperfections could be removed, leaving the totality the same or even improved. Imperfections in a part often contribute to the perfection of the whole; for, when many rules must be satisfied at once to achieve a generalized perfection, the rules often contravene each other and force exceptions which are impossible to avoid; hence imperfections will appear in the parts, which nevertheless contribute the greatest possible perfection to the whole. The human eye, for example, could never see the tiniest parts of an object without losing sight of the whole; if our eyes were microscopes, we would see a few points quite distinctly, but we would lose the totality. It is, therefore, necessary for our sight to be less distinct so that it can be matched to our needs, since distinguishing the least parts and the sight of the whole cannot be united; for, it is more useful for us to see the whole object than to distinguish all its points in turn: thus, it is an illusion to believe that the eye of man could have been more perfect, if it could see the tiniest parts of things, since seeing this way would have been basically useless for us.

The general will of God doubtless leads to the best and to the perfection of each particular thing; but his consequent will, which is the result of all his antecedent wills, and which cannot be executed in isolation, leads to the welfare and the greatest perfection of the whole, to which the perfection of parts must be subordinated.

It is true that we cannot see the entire tableau of the universe, or demonstrate in detail how the perfection of the whole results from the apparent imperfections we find in some of its parts; since this would require the ability to represent the entire universe for ourselves and compare it with all other possible universes, which is an attribute of the Deity. But, our powerlessness on this point cannot make us doubt that the supreme intelligence chose the best of all possible worlds to give existence to it; for, the necessary being, who is self-sufficient, who has no need for anything external, could not have considered any other end in the creation of this universe than to communicate a portion of his perfections to his creatures, and make something worthy of himself, since he would be failing himself, and even falling short of his own perfections, if he produced a world unworthy of his own wisdom.

A result of the concatenation of the parts and the whole is that not all imperfection can be removed from man. Man is a finite being, by his essence contained and limited within the totality. How many evils truly befall us because our understanding is limited, because we cannot know everything, understand everything, or be in all places where our presence is required? These are faculties which the creature could never possess without becoming a God. Thus, the imperfections in the creature are an effect of its limitations, they are necessary imperfections.

It follows, from all that I have just said, that the Supreme Being is infinitely good; for, having decided to create a world in order to share a part of his infinite perfections with it, he decided to grant actuality to the best possible series of things. He granted to each particular thing as much by way of essential perfection as it could accept; and he directed, by his wisdom, the evils that were inevitable in this series of things, to greater goods.

He is infinitely powerful; for, since God saw all that is possible from all eternity, his understanding is the source of all possibility, and since nothing could ever become possible but what God has conceived as such, and nothing could be realized except what he wished to grant existence to, he is the principle of possibility, of actuality, of all that is actual and possible.

God is the absolute master of this series of things to which he has granted existence; he can change and annihilate it; and, just as it's been shown that a contingent being cannot give existence to itself, or keep it for a single moment by its own force. Therefore, the reason for its continued existence cannot lie in the creature, which can neither have a beginning, nor continue to exist, except by the will of the creator, of which it has need at every moment for its maintenance in the actuality which he granted to it.

ON LIBERTY

The question of liberty is the most interesting one we can examine, since it might be said that on this one question depends all of morality.

A matter of such interest deserves a moderate departure from my subject to enter this discussion, and to place before the reader's eyes the principal objections made against liberty so that he can judge their solidity for himself.

I know that liberty has illustrious opponents, I know that arguments are made against it which might seem seductive initially, but these very arguments engage me to share and refute them.

Such obscurity has been brought into this subject that it is absolutely indispensable to begin by defining what is meant by liberty when we intend to discuss it, and make ourselves understood.

A DEFINITION OF LIBERTY.

I call *liberty a thing's power of thinking, of moving, or of not moving, according to the choice of its own mind.*

All the objections of those who deny liberty can be reduced to four principal ones, which I will examine, each in their turn.

THE 1ST OBJECTION OF THE FATALISTS AGAINST LIBERTY

Their first objection tends to weaken the witness of our conscience and of the inner sense we have of our liberty. They claim that it's only for lack of attention about what goes on inside us that we believe we have this intimate feeling, and that when we consciously attend to the causes of our actions, we find, on the contrary, that they are always necessarily determined.

In addition, we cannot doubt that there are motions in our bodies which are not dependent on our will, such as the circulation of blood, the beating of our hearts, etc. Often, too, anger, or some other violent passion carries us away and make us do things that our reason disavows. So many crushing visible chains prove, they say, that we are similarly bound in all other things.

Man, they say, *is often carried away so quickly and with shocks whose agitation and violence he feels, and often he is led by a peaceful movement which he doesn't notice, but to which he is no less subject. He's a slave who doesn't always feel the weight and encumbrance of his irons, but who is no less a permanent slave.*

THE RESPONSE

This argument is very similar to this one: *Men are sometimes sick; therefore, they are never healthy.* But who fails to see, on the contrary, that to be aware of one's disease and one's slavery is evidence that one was previously healthy and free.

In a state of intoxication, in the rush of a violent passion, when organs are out of order, etc., our will is no longer obeyed by our senses, and we are no more free to use our liberty than we would be to move a paralyzed arm.

Freedom in man is the health of the soul. Few enjoy this health entirely and unalterably, our liberty is weak and limited like all our other faculties, we strengthen it through the habit of reflecting on it, and mastering our passions, and this exercise of the soul renders it a little more vigorous. But whatever efforts we may make, we can never attain a state where our reason will be sovereign over all our desires, and there will always be involuntary movements in our soul, as in our body, for we are only wise, free, healthy, etc., to a very small extent.

I know that it's entirely possible to abuse one's reason to contest the liberty of animals, and conceive of them as machines without sensations or desires, or willpower, although they have all the indices of such things; I know that systems, that is, errors, can be forged to explain their nature, but in the end when we must interrogate ourselves, we are forced to confess, if we're honest, that we have a will, that we have the power to act, to move our body, to apply our mind to certain thoughts, to suspend our desires, etc.

Therefore, the enemies of freedom must confess that our inner sense assures us of our freedom; and I'm not afraid to claim that nobody doubts their own freedom in good faith, whose conscience doesn't resist the artificial feeling by which they would convince themselves that they act by necessity in all their actions. Thus, they are not content to deny this inner feeling of freedom, but they go still further.

SECOND OBJECTION: OUR INNER FEELING OF OUR LIBERTY MISLEADS US.

Even if we granted, they say, *that you actually have the inner feeling of liberty, this still wouldn't prove anything, because your inner feeling misleads you about your freedom, just as your eyes trick you about the size of the Sun when they make you think that the size of this star is about two feet wide, although its diameter is really about 100:1 relative to the Earth.*

This is what I think can be said in response to this objection.

RESPONSE.

The two cases you are comparing are quite different; I neither can nor should I see any objects except in direct relation to their size, and opposite the square of their distance. These are the mathematical laws of optics, and this is the nature of my organs, since, if my sight could perceive the real size of the Sun, I might be unable to see any object on Earth, and this sight, far from being useful to me, would instead be harmful. It's the same with the senses of hearing and smelling; I neither have nor can I have these sensations more or less strong (all things being equal) except as sonorous or odiferous bodies are more or less close to me. Thus, God did not deceive me by showing me that which is distanced from me by a size proportionate to its distance; but if I believe myself to be free, and I am not, then God must have created me only to trick me, since our actions seem free to us precisely as they would seem if we truly were. All that remains, then, for those who maintain the negative is the mere possibility that we are made in such a way that we are always invincibly deceived about our liberty; however, isn't this possibility based on an absurdity, since this perpetual illusion that God would give us would mean that the supreme being acts in a way that would be unworthy of his infinite wisdom.

And, let it not be said that it is unworthy of a philosopher to have recourse to God on this point, for, once this God has been proved, it is certain that he is the author of my liberty, if I am free, and that he is the author of my error if, having made me a purely passive being, he gave me the irresistible opinion of a liberty which he has denied to me.

This internal feeling we have of our freedom is so strong that, to make us doubt it, we would at least need a demonstration proving to us that there's a contradiction in the idea that we're free. And to be sure, there is no such demonstration.

Added to all these reasons which destroy the objections of the fatalists, even they are obliged to constantly contradict their opinion with their behavior. For, the most specious possible arguments can be made against our freedom, but we will always behave as if we were free, since the inner sense of our freedom is so deeply engraved in our soul, and since it is so influential, despite our prejudices, on our actions.

3RD OBJECTION: OUR UNDERSTANDING ALWAYS FOLLOWS WHATEVER SEEMS BEST TO IT, AND THIS DUTY OF OUR UNDERSTANDING SURELY DETERMINES OUR WILL.

Driven into this trench, those who deny freedom persist, and say that *This inner feeling, of which you say so much, assures you, it's because the motions of your body, and the thoughts of your mind, obey your will. But this will itself is always necessarily determined by things that your understanding judges as best, just as a balance always tilts to the greater weight. This is how the links of your chain hold onto each other.*

Our ideas, both from sensation and from reflection, present themselves to you whether you wanted them or not. For, you don't make your own ideas. And, when two ideas present themselves to your understanding, such as, for example, the idea of lying down and the idea of taking a walk, it's absolutely necessary, either for you to have desired one of these two things, or not to have desired either thing. You are not, therefore, free as to the act of wanting itself. In addition, it is certain that if you yourself chose, you would surely decide to go to bed or take a walk as your understanding judges one of these things as being useful or suitable for you. And, your understanding cannot help but judge as good and suitable, that which seems so to it. There are always differences in things, and these differences necessarily condition your judgment, for it would be impossible for us to choose between two things that are indiscernible (if anything really were). Therefore, all of our actions are necessary, since by your own confession, you always act in harmony with your will, and I have just proved 1) That your will is necessarily determined by the judgment of your understanding. 2) That this judgment depends on the nature of your ideas; 3) That, in the end, your ideas aren't dependent on you at all. Since this argument, in which the enemies of freedom find their principal strength, has many branches, there are also many responses.

Firstly, when it's said that we are not free as to the very act of willing, this relates in no way to our liberty, for freedom consists in acting or not acting, and not in willing or not willing.

Secondly, *our understanding*, it's said, *cannot help judging as good whatever seems that way, the understanding therefore determines the will,* etc. This argument is based only on the fact that we unconsciously produce so many little beings of understanding and will, which are assumed to act upon each other, and then condition our actions. But this is a misunderstanding which only needs to be seen to be corrected, for it's easy to sense that wishing, judging, etc., are only different functions of our understanding. In addition, to have perceptions, and to judge that something is true and reasonable when we see that it effectively is, not an action, but a simple passion, for it is indeed only to feel what we feel, and see what we see, yet there is no connection between the approbation and action, between what is passive and what is active.

Thirdly, *the differences of things condition*, they say, *our understanding.* But it is not considered that the liberty of indifference before the dictates of the understanding is a true contradiction in things which have real differences between them. For, according to this fine definition of freedom, idiots, imbeciles, even animals would be freer than we are, and we would be all the freer as we have fewer ideas, as we see fewer differences between things, in other words, in proportion with our stupidity, which is absurd.

If liberty is what we lack, I fail to see that we have much to complain about. Liberty of indifference in discernible things is not, therefore, real freedom.

With respect to the ability to choose between perfectly similar things, since we don't know them, it is hard for us to say what will then happen to us. I don't even know if this power would be a perfection, but what is quite certain is that the power, the self-moving, sole and true source of liberty, could only be destroyed by the indiscernibility of two objects. And, as long as man has this self-moving power, man will be free.

Fourthly, *as for the fact that our will is always determined by whatever our understanding judges as best,* I reply: *The will, that is, the final perception or approbation of the understanding* (for that is this word's meaning in the objection at hand); the will, I repeat, can have no influence over the self-moving power in which liberty consists. Thus, the will is never the cause of our actions, although it is their occasion, for an abstract notion can have no physical influence over the self-moving physical power which is inherent in man, and this power is exactly the same after the last judgment of the understanding.

It is true that there would be a contradiction in terms, morally speaking, in supposing that a wise being would commit a folly, and that, by consequence, it will surely prefer whatever its understanding judges as superior. But there would be no physical contradiction, for physical necessity and moral necessity must be carefully distinguished. The 1st is always absolute, but the 2nd is only ever contingent, and it is very compatible with the most perfect natural and physical liberty.

The physical power of acting is, therefore, what makes man a free being, however he may use it, and the deprivation of this power alone would suffice to make him a purely passive being, despite all his intelligence. For, if I throw a stone it would be an equally passive being, even if it had the internal sensation of motion that I pass to it.

Finally, to be conditioned by that which seems best to us is, at least, a perfection equal to the power of doing what we have judged to be such.

We have the faculty of suspending our desires, and of examining what seems best in order to choose it. This is a part of our liberty. The power of subsequent action in keeping with our choice is what renders this liberty full and entire, and it's by misusing our power of suspending our desires and by making decisions too quickly that we make so many mistakes. The better reasons our determinations are based on, the closer we come to perfection, and it's this perfection, in a more eminent degree, that characterizes the freedom of beings more perfect than us and that of God himself.

For, let there be no mistake: God can only be free in this way, the moral necessity of always doing what is best is only greater in God as his infinitely perfect being is above ours. The true and only liberty is, therefore, *the power of doing what one chooses to do*, and all these objections against this kind of liberty militate equally against that of God and of man, and if it follows that man is not free because his will is always determined by whatever his understanding judges best, it would also follow that God would not be free, and that everything would be an effect without a cause in the universe, which is absurd.

Man is, therefore, by his quality as an intelligent being with a need to want whatever his judgment shows him to be superior, if things were different, he would have to be subject to the conditioning of someone other than himself, and he would no longer be free, for, to want something that wouldn't bring pleasure is a true contradiction, *and to do what one judges best, which pleases most,* is to be free. We could hardly conceive of a being as being freer except as it is capable of doing what it wants, and, as man has this freedom, "as free, as it is possible for freedom to make him", in Locke's terms.

Finally, the *Achilles heel* of the enemies of liberty is the following argument.

4TH OBJECTION: GOD'S FOREKNOWLEDGE.

God is omniscient; past, present, and future are equally present to his eyes. And, if God knows all that I will do, then I must be absolutely determined to act in the way he foresaw, therefore our actions are not free. For if some future things were contingent or uncertain, if they depended on human liberty, in a word, if they may or may not happen, then God could not foresee them, and therefore, he would not be omniscient.

There are many other responses to this argument which initially seems unassailable.

RESPONSE.

1) God's foreknowledge has no influence on things' manner of existence. This foreknowledge gives things no more certainty than they would have had if there were no foreknowledge, and if the impossibility of human freedom is not established by other arguments, the mere consideration of the certainty of his Divine foreknowledge would not be able to destroy this liberty. For, God's foreknowledge is not the cause of the existence of things, but is rather based on their existence. Everything that exists today cannot fail to exist while it exists, and it was yesterday and from all eternity as certainly true as the things that exist today must exist, as it is now certain that these things exist.

2nd. The mere foreknowledge of some action before it occurs differs in no way from knowledge of it after the fact. Thus, foreknowledge changes nothing in the certainty of the event, since, if we grant for a moment that man is free, and that his actions cannot be foreseen, this would not imply the same certainty of occurrence in the nature of things, and in spite of liberty, would it not be, from yesterday and all eternity, equally certain that I would do a certain thing today, as there now is that I did this thing? Thus, whatever difficulty may have lied in imagining how God's foreknowledge contains only a certainty of the event which is always in things, even when they are not foreseen, it is evident that no necessity is entailed, and that it doesn't ruin the possibility of freedom.

God's foreknowledge is precisely the same as his knowledge. Thus, just as his knowledge has no influence over things which presently are, in the same way foreknowledge has no influence over those which are to come, and if freedom is actually possible, God's power of infallibly judging free events cannot make them become necessary, since, in this case, an action would have to be free and necessary at the same time.

3rd. It is truly impossible for us to conceive how God can foresee future things unless we posit a chain of necessary causes, for, to agree with the Scholastics that all is present to God not in truth *in mensura propria sed in mensura aliena, not in its own measure but in another measure,* this would introduce comedy into the most important question that we can debate.

It is far better to confess that the difficulties that we find in reconciling God's foreknowledge with our freedom stems from our ignorance about God's attributes, not an absolute incompatibility between foreknowledge and freedom. For, harmonizing God's foreknowledge with our freedom is no more incomprehensible to us than his Ubiquity, his infinite past duration, his infinite duration yet to come, and so many things which it will always be equally impossible for us to deny and to know, which we can neither deny nor know. The attributes of the supreme being are abysses where our feeble lights are useless. We do not and cannot understand the relationship between the foreknowledge of the creator and the liberty of the creature, and as the great Newton says: *ut coecus ideam non habet colorum, sic nos ideam non habemus modorum quibus Deus sapientissimus sentit et intelligit omnia*, which means: *just as the blind have no idea of colors, so we cannot comprehend how the infinitely wise being sees and knows all things.*

4th. But I would also ask those who deny human liberty on consideration of the divine foresight, whether God was able to create free creatures; they must reply that he could, since God can do anything, except what is contradictory, and only the attributes to which the ideas of necessary existence and absolute independence are attached, the communication of which involves a contradiction, and liberty is certainly not in this case, for otherwise, it would be as impossible for us to believe ourselves free as to believe ourselves infinite, omnipotent, etc. We must, therefore, either confess that God could create free beings, or say that he is not omnipotent, which, I think, nobody will say. Therefore, if God could create free beings, we can assume that's what he did, and if creating free beings and foreseeing their determinations involved a contradiction, then how could God, in creating free beings, be unaware of the use they would make of the freedom he gave them? It's no limitation to the divine power to limit it only to contradictions or creating free creatures, and upset their determinations in any way; it is, rather, a contradiction in terms. For, this would mean creating free and unfree creatures at the same time. Thus, it necessarily follows from God's power of creating free beings, that he either created beings such that his foreknowledge wouldn't destroy their liberty, or that he doesn't foresee their actions, and anyone who, on this supposition, would deny God's foreknowledge, would no more deny his all-knowingness than he who says that God cannot do whatever involves a contradiction denies his omnipotence.

But we are not reduced to this supposition. For, it is not necessary for me to understand how foreknowledge and liberty are compatible in order to accept both things. It's enough for me to be assured that I am free, and that God foresees all that must happen, for then, I must conclude that his omniscience and his foreknowledge don't ruin my freedom, although I cannot conceive how that can be, just as when a God is proved to me, I am obliged to accept the creation *ex nihilo* even though it's impossible for me to imagine it.

5th. If this argument of God's foreknowledge had any force against human freedom, it would also and equally destroy that of God. For, if God foresaw all that will happen, it is not therefore in his power to avoid doing what he foresaw himself doing, and it has been demonstrated that God is free. Freedom is therefore possible; God therefore could give his creatures a small portion of liberty, just as he gave them a small portion of intelligence.

WHAT DIFFERENCE THERE IS BETWEEN THE LIBERTY OF GOD AND THAT OF MAN, BETWEEN THE LIBERTY OF MAN, AND THAT OF THE ANIMALS.

Freedom in God is the power of always thinking what he wants, and always doing everything he wants. The freedom given from God to man is the feeble and limited power of performing certain movements and applying himself to certain thoughts. The freedom of children who aren't yet capable of reflection, and that of the unthinking animals, consists only in wanting and performing certain movements. If we were always free, we would be like God. So, let us therefore be content with a share suitable to the rank we hold in nature, but even though we lack the attributes of a God, let's not renounce the faculties of a man.

TRANSLATOR'S PREFACE TO MANDEVILLE'S *FABLE OF THE BEES*

1735

Ever since I began to live with myself, and to consider the worth of time, the brevity of life, and the futility of what usually consumes it, I have been astonished to notice how extremely careful I'd been with my teeth, my hair, while at the same time neglecting my mind and my understanding. I've realized that the mind rusts faster than iron, and that it's even harder to restore its original polish.

Such sensible thoughts cannot give the soul the suppleness, which it loses by lack of exercise, when one's youth has passed. The Indian Fakirs lose the use of their arm muscles because they leave them in the same posture and don't use them at all. We also lose our ideas when we neglect to cultivate them. This is a fire that dies out, unless it's continually given sustaining wood. Wishing therefore to make up, if possible, for such a great defect, and try to straighten a tree that's already so far grown, and make it produce the fruits that it should still produce, I have sought some kind of occupation that might, by fixing my mind, give it this consistency (if I may express myself in this way) which is never acquired when no goal is set in one's studies. We must direct ourselves, as in civic life, to have a good idea of what we want to be. Lack of resolution produces, in the former, false steps, and in the latter, confused ideas.

Those who have received an obvious talent from nature, only need to let themselves be led by the impulse of their genius, but there are few souls whom it leads by the hand, into the field they must either clear or beautify. There are even fewer of these sublime geniuses who carry within themselves the seed of all talents, and whose superiority can do anything successfully. Those who might have the best claims to this universal monarchy of the fine arts, however, can more easily attain perfection in a single one, and make it their favorite. Mr. de Voltaire, for example, although a great metaphysician, a great historian, a great philosopher, etc., has given preference to poetry, and the epithet "the greatest French poet" will also be his distinguishing characteristic as well as "a universal man".

It sometimes happens that labor and study force genius to declare itself, as when fruits are made to blossom artificially in a plot of land for which nature never made them, but these efforts of art are nearly as rare as natural genius. Most of those who think, for everyone else is a separate species, have to seek their talent within themselves. They know the difficulties of each art, and the failings of those who practice them, but undeterred courage and the superiority which helps one break through, has been refused them. Mediocrity is, even among the elect, the lot of the majority. Some are busy pruning thorns that would slow the progress of the true geniuses, and this is the job of so many dictionaries, and works of this kind which are so useful in literature. Certainly, colors must be ground up for the great painters. Others periodically give a report to the public of all that happens in the republic of letters. Finally, others transmit from one country to another, the discoveries and thoughts of great men, and remedy this misfortune, as far as they can, of the multiplicity of languages, so often deplored by all true lovers of the art.

I know that one does a greater service to one's country by producing riches taken from its own resources than by informing it of foreign discoveries, and that van Robais was more useful to France than he who brought it the first English sheets. But we must try to promote what little has been received as our lot and not fall into despair because one has only two acres to cultivate while others have ten leagues in the countryside.

We might apply to the arts this passage from the Gospel: *sunt plures mansiones in domo patris mei.* It is certainly better to provide a good translation of a respected English or Italian book than to write a bad one in French.

Translators are the traders in the Republic of Letters and they deserve, at least, praise for sensing and understanding their own forces, and for refraining from producing books by themselves, and carrying a burden that would crush them. Besides, if their work doesn't require that creative genius which certainly holds primacy in the empire of the fine arts, it requires such diligence that their knowledge must be appreciated all the more as they expect less glory for it.

Among all books, those of reasoning seem the most susceptible of good translations. Reason and morality belong to all countries. The genius of language, this bane of translators, is less noticeable in books where only ideas have to be conveyed, and where style is not the first merit, whereas works of imagination can be rarely transmitted from one people to another, for, in order to translate a good poet, you would nearly have to be as good a one as he.

Now, if it is impossible to have the faithful memorials of the human imagination, it is still possible to have some of their reason, and this is one of the debts we owe to translators. Thus, if human nature in general is indebted to wise Mr. Locke for teaching it to know the best part of itself, its Understanding, the French also owe something to Mr. Coste for introducing them to this great philosopher. Indeed, how many people, even among Locke's readers, don't know the English language, and how few among those who have learned this language of modern philosophy, would be in a position to understand Mr. Locke in English, and simultaneously overcome the difficulties of this language and those of the subject matter?

One must, no doubt, to resolve oneself to translating, be quite assured that it's for the commenters and not the translators who have been made to say in the temple of taste:

> *Taste is nothing, we are in the habit*
> *Of setting down at length, point by point*
> *All that is thought, but we ourselves don't think.*[4]

The judicious author of this charming work had a keen sense of the difference between composing large volumes on a passage from Dictys of Crete which nobody understands and which is a propos of nothing, or to appropriate for his own country the labors and discoveries of all others.

But, since everything is abused, the desire to make money and to be published has produced nearly as many bad translations as there are bad books.

If a good translation is not without some difficulties, it should at least seem easy to choose a good book as one's object. However,

---

[4] From Voltaire's *Le Temple du Goût.*

translations often come when the original has already been forgotten. The English suffer this inconvenience even more often than we do. There are no bad French books that they won't translate, witness *Sethos* and so many others. However, the profound genius of the English must make them less avid about our books, which are largely frivolous, by comparison with their own. What the earl of Roscommon said of our verses doesn't seem applicable to French books:

> *The weighty Bullion of one Sterling Line,*
> *Drawn to French Wire, would thro' whole Pages*

shine.

I believe that what makes translations so common among the English is that, since the French language is part of their education, more of them are able to translate.

There are many unfaithful translators, some, translating word for word, become unfaithful in their fear of being so. Others, find it difficult to grasp the meaning of their author, go wrong, and obscure a luminous thought which their mind only managed to glimpse. As for those who set their own nonsense in the place of those of the author they are translating, I consider travelers who abuse the proverb: *he who comes from afar can easily lie.* However, I believe that only translators of Oriental languages indulge in such things.

The difficulties of each art are for artists what the minutiae of events are for contemporaries. The interest they take in them and the point of view from which they see them, magnify the objects for both parties. Posterity and the public judge things quite differently. Thus, although it is true to say that a good translation requires diligence and effort, it is also certain that the best one is a very mediocre piece of work.

However, as mediocre as this kind of literature may be, it might still be thought very brazen for a woman to undertake it. I feel the full weight of prejudice which so universally excludes us from the sciences, and this is one of the most astonishing contradictions in this world for me, since there are large countries whose law allows us to decide their future, but none where we are raised to think.

A reflection on this prejudice which is quite singular is that acting is the only profession requiring any study and mental cultivation where women are allowed, and at the same time it's the only one that is declared scandalous.

Let's think a little about why, after so many centuries, never has a good tragedy, a good poem, a respected history, a good painting, a good book on physical science come from the hands of women? Why should these creatures, whose understanding seems so completely similar to that of men, seem however to be kept behind the barrier by an invincible power? Tell me if you can. I leave it to the naturalists to seek a physical explanation, but until they find it, women will have a right to protest about their education. For my part, I confess that if I were king, I would carry out this physical experiment. I would reform an abuse that prunes away, so to speak, half of humanity. I would have women participate in all the rights of humanity, especially those of the mind. It seems they were born to be tricked, and their minds are only allowed this kind of exercise. This new education would be a great boon for humanity in every way. Women would become more deserving and men would gain a new object for emulation and our commerce which, by polishing their minds, too often weakens and shrinks it, would then serve only to expand their knowledge. I will surely be told that I should ask the Abbott de St. Pierre to add this project into his planning. It might seem difficult to execute, although it might be more reasonable.

I am convinced that many women either ignore their talents, thanks to the defects of their education, or bury them from prejudice and a lack of intellectual courage. What I myself have felt has confirmed this opinion for me. Chance led me to make the acquaintance of men of letters who became my friends, and I was extremely shocked when they paid me any attention at all. I then started to believe that I was a thinking creature. But I only caught a glimpse of this, while society, frivolity, for which only I thought I was born, filled all my time and all my soul, and I didn't think of it seriously until I had come to an age when there is still time to become rational, but where the time has already passed for acquiring talents.

This thought did not discourage me. I still find myself thrilled to have renounced, in mid-course, the trifles that occupy most women their whole lives long, meaning in this way to use what remains thereof in cultivating my soul, and sensing that nature had refused me that creative genius which leads to the discovery of new truths, I have been fair to myself, and I have limited myself to rendering, with clarity, those which others have discovered, and which the diversity of languages render useless for most readers.

Having resolved to undertake this sort of work, my respect for the English and the taste I've always had for this philosophical nation's free and manly way of expressing itself, have led me to prefer their books over those of other nations, and I've chosen this book which has for its title *The Fable of the Bees* among all those that I might have translated, because it seems to me that this is one of all the books on earth that is most suitable for humanity in general. It is, I think, the best book of morality that has ever been written, that is, the one that leads men most to the true source of the views which nearly all of them follow without examination. Mandeville[5], its author, might be called the English Montaigne, except that his more methodical and has more sound ideas about things than Montaigne.

---

[5] He was the grandson of a French refugee. His example proves that French minds need to be transplanted to England to grow strong.

I don't have any idolatrous respect of all translators for my author. I confess that it is rather badly written in English, and that it sometimes runs on, and sometimes misses the mark, such as when it says that a thief is as useful to society as a bishop giving alms, and that there is no merit in saving from flames a child who's about to be devoured by them, and in many other parts, he says many things that are not true and which might be dangerous. I've taken care to apply correctives to these parts to avoid any potential danger. I've taken the liberty of pruning his style in many parts, and removing everything that relates only to the English, and is too uniquely connected to their customs.

I've also taken the liberty of adding my own thoughts, when the subject matter suggested to me that that they were worth the effort of writing. But, to keep them distinct from the text, I've indicated them with brackets.

Some thoughts in this book might seem a little brash, but, I think they are worth examining as to their truth, and if they teach men to know themselves, they cannot fail to be useful to men who think, which is the only purpose of this book. *Odi prophanum vulgus et arceo.*

I confess that, with my temerity in undertaking this work, I've also been bold enough to hope for success. I believe I am all the more obliged to give it my all, as success alone can justify me. At least, masculine injustice in excluding us from the sciences should serve to keep us from producing bad books. Let's try to have this advantage over them, and may this tyranny turn into a happy necessity for us, so that they will find nothing in our books to blame but our names.

ON THE RESURRECTION OF THE DEAD

from *Examens de la Bible*

This is one of the capital points of the Christian religion. It is also one of the most consoling, and one of the most absurd things that men have ever imagined. The ancients considered it a ridiculous opinion. St. Paul was mocked by the entire areopagus when he said that Jesus had been resurrected.

The Fathers have held various opinions on the resurrection. The millenarians believed that there would be two. But if there is one, there might as well be a thousand. This resurrection and this life to come save God from many missteps. For, if the just are persecuted, miserable, and few of them survive, if the Lord doesn't make good his most solemn oaths in the Old and New Testaments, then the future life responds to all these points, and makes up for everything. The Christians might have spared themselves the absurdity of the resurrection of the body; the immortality of the soul was adequate, along with allegories, for which they never lack, to save God's fairness and faithfulness; however, Jesus was resurrected bodily; they all want to resurrect like him.

When I say that the Christians could have made do without the resurrection, I'm referring to those who wrote the books that are accepted in the Church; and it is true that by following these books, acceptance of the resurrection is unavoidable.

This fine spectacle will begin with the sound of a trumpet. St. Paul, 2nd Thess., chapter 4, verses 15 and 16 and 1st Corinthians, chapter 15, verse 52, and J.C. in St. John, chapter 5, verse 8, and in St. Matthew, chapter 24, verse 51. It is said in these two evangelists that the son of man will send his angels with a trumpet and a thundering voice. However, the trumpet seems sufficient.

One subject of debate is the question of who will resurrect first, the elect or the wicked? Or will they all resurrect together? We can choose according to St. Paul, for he says, 1st Cor., chapter 15, verse 52, that we will all resurrect together, and in the same chapter 15, verse 23, he says that everyone will resurrect in due order; that is, according to one's merits; and the Christians will precede all others. It's also asked whether those who happen to be alive on the day of judgment will die. Again, according to St. Paul, we can also make a choice on this point: for he says to the Hebrews, chapter 9, verse 27, that *all men must die*; and to the Corinthians: *We will not all die, but we will all be changed*; aside from these questions which keep good Christians occupied, the heathens ask many others, harder still, which the Church dismisses, unable to respond. These questions concern the nature of the bodies, their size, their age, their sex? Will some be resurrected in infancy? In old age? Will monsters, miscarriages, abortions resurrect? Will the blind, eunuchs, etc., resurrect in their state of mutilation and deprivation? It's said that our bodies will be light, transparent, luminous. If they are material, as they must be in a material resurrection, this will massively diminish the weight pressing down on the earth; but there are cases where the resurrection will not be a favor. Is it worth the trouble, for example, to be resurrected at 9 months, at 6 weeks, or at the age of 100? There are some who believe that deaf and blind children, who died before the age of reason, will resurrect fully grown; but if children resurrect as adults, won't they be what they never were?

The bodies of the wicked, it is said, will not be changed. But those of the righteous will be changed, and for their own benefit; but if the bodies of the wicked are not changed, how will they resurrect unto eternal flames?

It's also questioned whether men and women will resurrect with their sex intact? The reply given is no, based on the response of J.C. in St. Matthew, chapter 22, verse 30, to the man who asked him whom the wife would belong to, after marrying 7 men, that, at the resurrection *there will be neither husband nor wife but they will all be like the angels of*

God in heaven. What will we do with a body, in a wholly intellectual paradise; with a mind like God which no sense can perceive? How can the parts of our body rediscover each other? The omnipotence of God replies here instead of reason.

Will animals be resurrected? Nobody knows about that; and yet it must be allowed: this shouldn't be any harder to know than the rest.

ON HAPPINESS

It is commonly thought that happiness is difficult to find, and we have only too many good reasons to think so; but it would be easier to become so, if people would precede their conduct with thought and a plan of action. We are driven by circumstances, and given to hopes which only ever pay us half of what we anticipate: ultimately, the means of happiness are only seen clearly when age and self-imposed hindrances have placed obstacles in their way.

Let us prevent such tardy reflections: those who read these ones will find in them all that age and the circumstances of their lives would only too slowly grant them. Let's keep from wasting part of the precious and short time that we have for feeling and thinking, and caulking our ship when we could be enjoying our trip.

Happiness requires freedom from prejudices, virtue, health, tastes and passions, a susceptibility to illusions, since we owe most of our pleasures to illusions, and woe to those who lose them. Far, then, from seeking to dispel them with the torch of reason, we should try instead to thicken the gloss it paints on most things; it is even more necessary for them than care and adornment are for our bodies.

We must begin by telling and convincing ourselves that we have no business in this world other than to procure pleasant sensations and feelings for ourselves. The moralists who tell humanity: *repress your passions and master your desires, if you want to be happy*, know nothing about the way to happiness. Happiness comes only through the satisfaction of our tastes and passions; we are not always lucky enough to have passions, and in the absence of passions, we must be content to have tastes. Therefore, passions are what we should ask of God, if we dare ask anything of him; and Le Notre was quite right to ask the Pope for temptations instead of indulgences.

But, you might ask, do the passions not make more people unhappy than happy? I don't have scales adequate to weighing up what good and evil they may have done to mankind in general; but it must be noted that the unhappy are known by the way they need others, that they love recounting their miseries to others, that they expect relief and comfort in so doing. Those who are happy, on the other hand, seek nothing, and don't go telling everyone about how happy they are; the unhappy are show-offs, the happy are anonymous.

This is why, when two lovers are reconciled, when their jealousy has passed, when the obstacles that separated them are overcome, they are no longer suitable as characters for the stage; the show is over for the spectators; and the scene between Renaud and Armide wouldn't be as interesting as it is, if the spectator didn't think that Renaud's love came by an enchantment which will fade, and that the passion shown by Armide in this scene will heighten the interest of their misfortune. The very same mechanisms affect our soul, moving it at theatrical representations and in life's events. Therefore, we are far better acquainted with from the aches it produces than from the happiness, so often obscure, which it brings to the lives of men. But, even assuming for a moment that the passions make more people unhappy than happy, I claim that they would still be desirable, since they are the condition *sine qua non* for enjoying the great pleasures; and life is only worth the trouble for the sake of pleasant feelings and sensations, and the more intense these feelings are, the happier we are. It is, therefore, desirable to be susceptible to passions, and, to repeat: not everyone who wants them enjoys their company.

It's up to us to use them for our happiness, which is an area we can often influence. Whoever has been so skilled in managing their condition and the circumstances of fate that he has managed to get his mind and heart into a place of stability which is susceptible to all the feelings, all the pleasant sensations this state can offer, is surely an excellent philosopher and owes a debt of gratitude to nature.

I say that his state and the circumstances where fate has placed him, because I believe that one of the things that contributes most to happiness is to be content in one's state, and try to render it happy rather than to change it.

My aim is not to write for every sort of condition and all sorts of people; not all states are capable of the same kinds of happiness. I only write for those who are called "society people", that is, those who have a ready-made fortune, somewhat impressive, somewhat opulent, but ultimately, one that allows them to rest easy as they are without any hardship; and such people may not be the easiest sort to render happy.

But, to have passions, to be able to satisfy them, certainly health must be enjoyed; this is the chief good. And, this good is not as independent of us as many seem to think. Since we are all born healthy (generally speaking) and made to exist for a certain duration, it is sure that if we don't ruin our temperament by gluttony, by late nights, essentially by excess, we will all live more or less to what is called "the age of man"; with the exception of violent deaths which one cannot foresee and which, consequently, are not worth worrying about.

But, you may ask, if your passion is gluttony then you must be quite miserable, for, to keep your health you must always practice restraint. To this I respond that, since happiness is your goal, through the satisfaction of your passions, you must let nothing get between yourself and this goal; and if the stomach aches or gout occasioned by your excesses at table bring you pains that are more intense than the pleasure you find in satisfying your gluttony, then you're miscalculating, if you prefer the enjoyment of the one over the deprivation of the other: you are missing your goal, and your unhappiness is your own fault. Don't pity yourself for being a glutton; this passion is a source of continual pleasures; but learn how to use it for your happiness: this will be easy for you if you stay at home, where only what you want to eat will be served: observe times of abstinence; if you leave your stomach until it desires with a true hunger, everything that appears will be as pleasurable as the more refined dishes, which you never think of when they aren't set in front of you. This self-imposed sobriety will intensify the pleasure. I don't recommend this for the sake of suppressing your gluttony at all, but only to prepare you for a more delightful enjoyment of it. As for those who are ill, or fragile natures upset by everything, they have other kinds of happiness. To feel very warm, to digest their chicken, to successfully walk to their wardrobe may bring them enjoyment. This sort of happiness, if it is one, is too bland to worry about how it is attained. It seems that these sorts of people are in a sphere which what we call happiness, enjoyment, pleasant feelings cannot approach. They are to be pitied; but nothing can be done for them.

When we are convinced that without health we can enjoy no pleasure and no other blessing, it's easy to accept a few sacrifices to preserve it. I can share a personal example here. I have a very good temperament, but I am not robust, and there are things that would surely destroy my health; Wine, for example, and all sorts of liquors; I have forbidden myself these things from my earliest youth. I have a fiery temperament, I spend my mornings drowning in liquids; ultimately, I indulge too often in the gluttony that God endowed me with; but I make up for this excess with rigorous diets which I impose on myself at the first signs of discomfort, and his has always staved off all illness. These diets cost me nothing, since, at such times, I stay home at dinner-time; and, since nature is wise enough to keep us from feeling hungry when we have eaten too much, since my gluttony is only stimulated by the sight of all the dishes, I'm refusing myself nothing by eating nothing, and I regain my health without any deprivation at all.

Another source of happiness is freedom from prejudice; and all this requires is that we get rid of them. We are all given enough intelligence to examine that which others would have us believe; to know, for example, whether two plus two equals four or five; besides, in this century, nobody lacks for help in educating themselves. I know that there are other prejudices than those of religion, which are quite good to shake off, although none of them influence our happiness or unhappiness more than those of religion. Prejudice is the same thing as an opinion accepted without examination, because it could not withstand it. Error can never be a good, and it is surely a great evil in matters of our behavior.

We must never confuse prejudice with decorum. Prejudices contain no truth, and can be useful only to crooked minds: some souls are corrupt, just as some bodies are deformed. They are disordered, and I have nothing to say to them. Decorum contains truths of convention, which should be enough for good men to follow them. There is no book teaching decorum, and yet nobody, at least those in good faith, is honestly ignorant on the subject. It varies with condition, age, circumstances. Nobody who aspires to happiness should ever dismiss it; the utmost observation of decorum is a virtue, and I said above that to be happy, you must be virtuous. I mean by *virtue* all that contributes to the happiness of society, and, consequently, to our own, since we are members of society.

I declare that we cannot be both happy and vicious, and the demonstration of this axiom lies in the bottom of all men's hearts. I maintain, even to the most wicked, that there is no man whose conscience, that is, his inmost feelings, the contempt he thinks he deserves and which he feels when he is discovered, doesn't play the role of torturer. By "wicked" I'm not referring to thieves, murderers, poisoners; such men aren't included in the category for whom I'm writing; but I give this name to those who are false and treacherous, slanderers, informers, ingrates, truly, all who are beset by vices against which the laws do nothing, but against which those of morals and society have issued decrees that are far worse, since they are always effective.

I maintain, then, that no-one on earth can feel that he is despised without despairing. This public contempt, this animadversion of good men, is a torture crueler than anything that the police lieutenant could ever inflict, since it lasts longer, and its victim is robbed of all hope.

And so, you cannot indulge in vice if you would avoid unhappiness; but it's not enough for us not to be unhappy; life would not be worth the trouble if all we could hope for was the absence of pain; annihilation would be better: for surely, this is the state of least suffering. And so, we should try to be happy. We must be on good terms with ourselves for the same reason that we have to be comfortably housed with ourselves, and it would be vain to hope to be able to enjoy this satisfaction without virtue:

> *Aisément des mortels on éblouit les yeux;*
> *Mais on ne peut tromper l'œil vigilant des*
dieux[6].

As one of our best poets said; we can never hide from the vigilant eye of our own conscience.

We hand out precise justice to ourselves, and the more we can say that we have fulfilled our duties, that we have done all the good we could

---

[6] "The eyes of mortals are easily dazzled; / But not so the vigilant eye of the Gods" Voltaire, *Semiramis*.

do, that we are, simply put, virtuous, the more we enjoy this inner satisfaction that can be called the health of the soul. I doubt whether there is any more delightful feeling than the one that comes in the wake of a virtuous deed, and which deserves the respect of upright men. Along with the inner pleasure caused by virtuous deeds comes the pleasure of universal respect: for, knaves cannot refuse to respect probity; the respect of the upright alone merits consideration.

Finally, I say that to be happy we must be susceptible to illusion, and this doesn't require proof; but, you'll say, you have said that error is always harmful: isn't illusion error? No: truly, illusion shows things to us completely as they must be to give us pleasant feelings, it adapts them to our nature. There are such things as optical illusions, but optics never tricks us, although it does not show us things as they are, since it shows them to us as we must see them for our own utility. Why do I laugh more than anyone else at puppet shows, if not because I am more susceptible than others to illusions, and within fifteen minutes I really think it's Punch who's talking? Would we enjoy a single minute of these shows if we weren't taken in by illusions presenting us with personalities we know to be long dead, and making them speak in alexandrine verse? And what enjoyment would we find in a show where all is illusion, if we couldn't be taken in? Surely there would be much at stake there, and those who only enjoy the music and dancing at the opera, are only enjoying it in an incorporeal manner, far beneath what is offered by the totality of this enchanting spectacle. I have cited these shows, because here illusion is more sensible. It blends in all the pleasures of our life, and provides a gloss for them. It might be said that it doesn't depend on us, which is only too true, up to a certain point; we can't give ourselves illusions, just as we can't choose our tastes, or passions; but we can preserve the illusions we do have; we can refrain from going backstage to gape at the wheels that make the characters fly, or the other machines: this is all the art that can be brought to the matter, and this art is neither useless nor fruitless.

Here, then, are the great machines of happiness, if I may be allowed this expression; but there are also more particular skills that can contribute to our happiness.

The first of all is to be entirely resolved about what one wants to be and what one wants to do, which most people lack; however, this is the condition *sine qua non* for happiness. Without this we continually swim in a sea of uncertainty; destroying in the morning what we made the night before; spending our whole lives doing stupid things, fixing them, regretting them.

This feeling of repentance is one of the most painful and unpleasant ones that our soul can experience. One of the great secrets is knowing how to safely prevent it. Since nothing is alike in life, it's nearly always useless to see one's own flaws; it is, at least, useless to pause for long in considering them and criticizing ourselves for them: it means covering our own eyes with confusion for no good reason. We set out from where we are, employing all the sagacity of our mind to correct and find ways to improve things; but we must not look back, and we must always free our mind from the memory of our faults: when we get, at first sight, whatever fruit might be expected, we may set aside all sad ideas and replace them with pleasant ones, this is another of the greatest sources of happiness, and that is in our power, at least to a certain point; I know that, in the midst of a violent passion that makes us unhappy, we can't completely banish every upsetting idea from our minds; but we aren't always in such overpowering situations, not all diseases are malignant; and the minor ailments, the unpleasant, albeit feeble, sensations, are worth avoiding. Death, for example, is an idea that always upsets us, whether foreseeing our own or thinking about those we love. We should, therefore, carefully avoid anything that might remind us of this idea. I'm quite opposed to Montaigne, who was so proud of being so accustomed to death that he was sure of meeting it without any fear. It's clear from his eagerness to share this victory that it cost him dearly, and wise Montaigne miscalculated on this point: for surely, it is folly to poison, with this sad and humbling idea, a portion of what little time we have for living, to more patiently endure a moment when physical pain will always make very bitter, in spite of our philosophy; besides, who knows if the weakening of our mind, caused by illness or age, will let us benefit from our reflections, and whether our efforts will be wasted, as often happens in life? Let's always keep in mind, when the idea of death returns, this verse of Gresset's:

Pain is a century, death is a moment.

Let's turn our minds away from every unpleasant idea; they are the source of all metaphysical suffering; and above all, we can nearly always choose to avoid them.

Wisdom should always keep her chips in her hand: for "wise" means "happy", at least in my dictionary; passions are necessary for happiness; but they must be put to use for our happiness, and some of them must be barred from entering our soul. I am not referring to passions that are vices, such as hatred, vengeance, or anger; ambition, for example, is a passion which I believe must be prohibited to the soul, if happiness is desired; not because it has no enjoyment, for I think this passion can bring that; it's not because ambition always has desires, for this is surely a great blessing; but since, of all the passions, this is the one that most makes our happiness dependent on others; and the less our happiness depends on others, the easier it is to be happy. We shouldn't fear to reduce this too far, it will always depend on them quite a lot. For this reason of independence, love of study is, of all passions, the one that contributes most to our happiness. This love of study contains a passion from which an elevated soul is not completely exempt: glory; half of the world can win glory in this way alone, and this is the same half whose education removes the means to it and renders a taste for it impossible.

It is certain that the love of study is far less necessary for man's happiness than for women's. Men have an infinity of resources for happiness that women lack entirely. They have many other paths to glory, and it is certain that a drive to put one's talents to use for one's country and to serve one's fellow citizens, either by one's skill in the art of war, or by their talents for government or trade, is far above anything we could expect to win through our studies. But women are excluded, by their state, from all kinds of glory; and when by chance a woman appears who was born with a very noble soul, her study is all she has to console her for all the exclusion and dependency to which she finds herself condemned by her state.

The love of glory, which is the source of so many pleasures for the soul and so many efforts of every kind which contribute to the happiness, education, and perfection of society, is based entirely on illusion; nothing could be easier than to dispel the phantom after which all noble souls chase; but what a loss this would be for them and for others! I know that there is some reality in the love of glory which can be enjoyed during one's life; but there is no hero, of any sort whatever, who cares nothing for the applause of posterity, from whom he expects even more justice than his contemporaries can offer. It's not always above the surface, this vague wish to be spoken of after one has gone; but it still remains at the bottom of our hearts. Philosophy would show the vanity of this; but feelings prevail; and this pleasure is no illusion, since it is proved by the real benefit of enjoying our future reputation; if the present were our only good, our pleasures would be far more limited than they are. We are happy in the present moment, not only because of our current enjoyments, but also because of our hopes and memories. The present is enriched by the past and the future. Who would work for their children, for the size of their house, without some enjoyment of the future? Whatever we may do, our self-love is always the more or less hidden motive of our actions; this is the wind that fills the sails, without which the ship would go nowhere.

I've said that the love of study is the most necessary passion for our happiness. This is a guaranteed resource against misfortune, it is a source of inexhaustible pleasures, and Cicero was quite right when he said that *the pleasures of sense and of the heart are doubtless inferior to those of study; it is not necessary to study to be happy; but it may well be necessary to study to have an inner sense of this resource and assistance.* We can love studying while going years, even our whole lives, without doing any study; and happy is he who goes through life this way! For it can only be to more vivid pleasures that he will sacrifice a pleasure which he is always sure to find, and which he will render more intense until it compensates for the loss of others.

One of the greatest secrets of happiness is to moderate your desires and love what you already have. Nature, whose aim is always our happiness (and by nature I mean all that relates to instinct and not reason); nature, I say, only gives us desires according to our condition; we naturally desire only one thing and then the next one; the infantry's Captain wants to be the Colonel, and he doesn't feel downcast because he's not the Commander, no matter what talents he sees in himself. Our mind and reflections must strengthen this wise sobriety of nature; we are only made happy through the satisfaction of desires; therefore, we must allow ourselves to desire only what can be obtained without excessive effort and struggle, and this is a point on which we can do much for our own happiness. Loving what we have, enjoying it, savoring the advantages of our position, keeping our gaze off those who seem happier than us, applying ourselves to the perfection of our own happiness and taking the fullest possible advantage of it, is what we should call happy; and I think I am offering a good definition of it by saying that the happiest of men is he who least desires a change of state. To enjoy this happiness, we must heal or prevent a disease of another kind which entirely opposes it, and which is only too common, that is, disquietude. This mental disposition opposes all our enjoyments, and consequently every kind of happiness. Good philosophy, that is, the firm conviction that we have nothing to do in this world other than to be happy, is a sure remedy against this disease from which good minds, those who are capable of principles and conclusions, are always exempt.

There is a highly irrational passion in the eyes of philosophers and reason itself, the motive of which, disguised as it may be, is even humiliating, and should suffice of itself to heal one of it, but which can also make one happy: this is the passion for gambling. It would be a good one to have, if it could be moderated and saved for the time of our lives where its help will be necessary, and this time is old age. It is certain that the love of gambling originates in the love of money. There is nobody for whom the big games (and I call a "big game" any that could make a difference in our wealth) isn't of interest. Our soul wants to be moved by hope or fear; it is only made happy by the things that make it feel alive. And, gambling constantly sets us against these two passions, and in this way it retains our soul in an emotion which is one of the great principles of our happiness. The pleasures of gambling have often consoled me for not being rich. I think my mind is well enough made that my fortune, although only mediocre as others see it, is enough to make me happy, and in this case gambling would seem dull; at least, this was my concern, and this idea convinced me that I owed the pleasure of gambling to my lack of great wealth, and served to console me for it.

It is certain that physical needs are the source of the sense pleasures, and I am convinced that there is more pleasure to be found in a moderate fortune than in a great abundance: a box, something made of porcelain, a new piece of furniture, are true pleasures for me but, if I have thirty boxes already, I would be quite insensitive to the pleasure of the thirty-first one. Our tastes are easily blunted by satiety, and we must thank God for giving us the deprivation necessary to preserve them. This is why a king is so often bored and why it is impossible for him to be happy, if heaven didn't give him a great enough soul to enjoy the pleasures of his condition, that is, to make many others happy; but then this state becomes preeminent in terms of happiness, as it is in terms of power.

I've said that the more our happiness depends on ourselves, the more secure it is; and yet, passion, which can bring us greater pleasures and make us happier, makes our happiness entirely dependent on others; I'm obviously referring to love. This passion may be the only one that can make us wish for life and make us thank the author of nature, whoever this may be, for granting us our existence. Lord Rochester was quite right to say that the gods placed this celestial drop in the chalice of life, to give us the courage to endure it:

We must love, for this is what sustains us:
For without love, 'tis sad to be human.

If this mutual taste, which is a sixth sense, and the most refined, delicate, and precious of all, happens to have gathered two souls that are equally sensitive to happiness and pleasure, then everything is ready, nothing else is required for happiness, nothing else matters; nothing but health is needed. We must use all the faculties of our soul to enjoy this happiness; we must depart life when this is lost, and be quite assured that the longevity of Nestor is nothing compared to fifteen minutes of such enjoyment as this. It is true that such happiness is rare; if it were common, it would be better to be human than divine, at least as we imagine God to be. The best we can do is to convince ourselves that this happiness is not impossible. However, I don't know whether love has ever brought together two people who were made so much for each other, that they never knew satiety of enjoyment, or the coolness that comes with security, or the indolence and blandness made by the ease and continuity of a commerce whose illusion is never broken (for where is there more of this than in love?), the ardor of which, finally, was equal in enjoyment and deprivation, and was able to endure misery and pleasure equally.

A heart capable of such love, such a tender and firm soul, seems to have exhausted the power of the Deity; only one is born in a century; it seems to have been beyond his power to make two, or, if he meant to produce them, he would have become jealous of their pleasures, if they ever met up. But love can make us happy at far lower cost: a tender and sensitive soul is made happy by the mere pleasure it finds in love. I don't mean to say that we can be made perfectly happy by love that is not returned; but I say that, although our ideas of happiness are not entirely satisfied by the love of our beloved, the pleasure we feel when we give in to all our tenderness, may be enough to make us happy; and if this soul is still lucky enough to be susceptible to illusions, it is impossible for it not to think it is loved more than it may truly be; it should love so much that it loves enough for two, and the warmth of its heart should make up for whatever is really lacking in its happiness. No doubt, a sensitive, lively, and passionate character will have to pay for the drawbacks related to these qualities, and I can't say whether I should say good or bad ones; but I think that whoever will compose themselves will bring them in. The initial passion carries a soul of this caliber so far outside itself that it is inaccessible to all reflection and all moderate ideas; it can certainly make preparations for great future sorrows; but the greatest drawback related to this passionate sensibility is that it is impossible for anyone who loves to this point of excess to find love, and there is hardly any man whose fondness isn't diminished by awareness of such a passion. This must no doubt seem rather odd to those whose understanding of the human heart is limited, but, for what little we attend to experience, we will sense that, if we would hold a lover's heart for long, he must always be affected by hope and fear. And, a passion of the sort I've just described produces an abandonment of oneself, rendering them incapable of any skillful action. Love stabs on every side: they begin by adoring you; it's impossible to be otherwise; but soon the certainty of love, and the bother of being constantly frustrated, the misfortune of having nothing to fear, deaden the desire. This is what the human heart is made of, and don't think I'm speaking from bitterness: God gave me, true enough, one of those tender and unchanging hearts that can't hide their feelings or moderate their passions, which never know either weakness or distaste, whose tenacity can overcome anything, even the certainty of unreturned love; but I have been kept happy for ten years by the love of someone who conquered my soul; and, during these ten years, I have conversed with him without a moment of aversion or boredom. When age, illness, perhaps also satiety with our pleasures diminished his fondness, I was slow to realize it; I was loving for two, I spent my whole life with him; and my heart, free from suspicion, enjoyed the pleasure of loving and the illusion of believing itself loved in return. It is true that I lost such a happy state, and that it cost me many tears.

Only savage thrashing can break such chains; the wound of my heart has bled for so long. I had a right to self-pity, and I have forgiven everything; I've been smart enough to see that perhaps nothing on earth but my heart could have this immutability which destroys the power of time; that, if age and disease had not fully extinguished his desires, they might still be available, and love would have led me back; finally, that, since his heart was incapable of love, he loved me with the dearest friendship and would have dedicated his life to me. My realization of the impossibility of regaining his fondness and passion, which I knew was not in nature's plan, has gradually led my heart to the tranquility of friendship; and this feeling, joined with the passion for study, made me quite happy.

But can such a tender heart truly be satisfied by a feeling as peaceful and feeble as friendship? I don't know if one should hope, or even wish to retain this sensibility forever, in the sort of apathy from which it was hard to separate it.

We are only made happy by strong and pleasant feelings. Why, then, would we deprive ourselves of the strongest and most pleasant ones of all? But what one has experienced, the reflections that were necessary to lead one's heart to this apathy, even the troubles required to reduce it to such a point, must make us afraid to depart from a state which is not an unhappy one, only to suffer misfortunes which age and the loss of beauty would render useless.

"Fine thoughts," you might say, "but useless ones!" You'll see how they could help, if you have ever felt a fondness for someone who fell in love with you. But I think it's misguided to call these thoughts useless. The passions, after thirty years, lose their power over us. Do you think anyone would resist their own taste, if it were so strongly desired and if one were fully convinced that it would make us miserable? We only give in to it because we aren't completely convinced of the certainty of these maxims, and we still hope to be happy, and we are right to think like this. Why forbid yourself all hope of happiness, of the most intense kind? But if we must not forbid ourselves this hope, nor are we allowed to deceive ourselves about the means to happiness; experience should, at least, teach us to count on ourselves, and use our passions for our happiness. We can take upon ourselves so much; we can't do everything, of course, but we can do plenty; and my claim, without any fear of mistake, is that there is no passion that can't be overcome, when we're fully convinced that it will only make us unhappy. What misleads us in our youth is the fact that we're incapable of reflection, lacking experience, and we imagine we can regain a lost advantage by simply running after it; while experience and knowledge of the human heart teach us that the more we chase it, the faster it flies away:

it's a false perspective which vanishes the moment we try to grab it. Taste is involuntary, something we cannot be talked into, and is almost never revived. What is your goal, when you give in to your yearning for someone? Is it not happiness from the pleasure of loving and being loved? As ridiculous, then, as it would be to refuse this pleasure, in fear of some future misfortune, which may only come after being very happy; and then there will be a compensation, and you should think about healing, and not regretting anything, a rational person should only blush if they didn't keep their happiness in their hands, and if they placed it entirely in those of another.

The great secret of keeping love from ruining our happiness is to try to never be in the wrong with your lover, to never seem overeager when he is cool with you, and always be cooler than he is; this won't bring him back; but then, nothing will, there is nothing to be done but to forget someone who stops loving you. If he still loves you, nothing can heat things up and restore his affection to the way it was the first time around, but the fear of losing you and being loved less. I know that this secret is hard for tender and true souls to practice; but they cannot try too hard to practice it, especially because it is far more necessary for them than anyone else. Nothing is more degrading than the measures taken to win back a cold or a faithless heart: they debase us in the eyes of the man we would keep, and those of other men who might think about us; but worse still, it makes us unhappy and torments us for no purpose.

We must, therefore, follow this maxim with unwavering courage, and never submit on this point to our own heart; we must try to know the character of the person we are attached to, before giving in to our fondness; our reason must be taken into consideration, not that reason which condemns all commitment as contrary to happiness, but that which, by agreeing that nobody can be very happy without love, counsels us to love only for the sake of our happiness, and rise above an inclination where we foresee nothing but misery.

But when this fondness prevails, when it has defeated our reason, which is only too common, there is no benefit in boasting of a steadfastness that would be both absurd and out of place. This is a great chance to practice the proverb: *the shortest follies are the best ones*;

these are, above all, the briefest miseries; for, there are some follies that would make us very happy only if they lasted a lifetime We must not be embarrassed about a misstep; we must heal ourselves, whatever the cost, and above all, avoid the presence of an object that can only get us worked up, and make us lose the fruit of our meditations: for, with men, flirting promotes love; they don't want to lose their conquests or victories, and with countless flirtatious acts they can relight a fire that's not quite dead, and keep you in a state of uncertainty that is as ridiculous as it is unbearable. Cut things off, make a clean break; we must, says Richelieu, *unstitch friendship and tear up love*; finally, it's the province of reason to make us happy: in childhood, only our senses carry this burden; when we're young, the heart and the mind begin to intervene, with this subordination where the heart decides everything; but at the age of maturity, reason must participate, it's the business of reason to show us that we must be happy, whatever it takes. Every age has its own pleasures; those of old age are the hardest to obtain; *gaming* and *study*, if this is still possible, *food*, *respect*: these are the resources of old age. These are all, to be sure, only consolations: fortunately, all we have to do is move the end of our lives forward, if it is too long in coming; but, as long as we are resolved to endure to the end, we must try to bring in pleasure by every door leading to our soul; we truly have no other business.

Let us try, then, to be healthy, to have no prejudices, to enjoy our passions, to use them for our happiness, to replace our passions with tastes, to carefully preserve our precious illusions, to be virtuous, to never repent, to cast off all sad ideas, and never allow our heart to keep an ounce of fondness for someone whose own fondness vanishes and who stops loving us. We must truly bid farewell to love one day, if we age at all, and this day should be the one when it ceases to make us happy. Finally, let us cultivate our fondness for study, this fondness which keeps our happiness dependent only on ourselves. Let us avoid ambition, and especially let us be entirely cognizant of what we want to be; let us be resolute on the path we wish to take to spend our lives there, and try to plant flowers along the way.

Made in the USA
Las Vegas, NV
18 December 2021